little book **BIG idea**

What is music?

NoodleJUICE

Noodle Juice Ltd
www.noodle-juice.com
Stonesfield House, Stanwell Lane, Great Bourton, Oxfordshire, OX17 1QS
First published in Great Britain 2023
Copyright © Noodle Juice Ltd 2023
Text by Noodle Juice 2022 • Illustrations by Katie Rewse 2022
All rights reserved
Printed in China
A CIP catalogue record of this book is available from the British Library.
ISBN: 978-1-915613-16-5
1 3 5 7 9 10 8 6 4 2

What is music?

Music is unique to humans; it isn't made by anything else in the animal world. But what – EXACTLY – is music? How do we know what is music, and what isn't?

Let's ask some questions to see if we can work it out!

So what makes a piece of music?

When did music start?

What is a song?

Are there different types of music?

What are musical instruments?

What is a choir?

What is an orchestra?
(Page 16)

What is a composer?
(Page 18)

Is music the same all around the world?
(Page 20)

Have computers changed the world of music?
(Page 22)

What can you do with music?
(Page24)

How can music help people?
(Page 26)

So what makes a piece of music?

Music can be happy or sad, fast or slow. Tunes can be played on instruments or sung by singers in a choir or pop group.

Music is usually a **melody** or tune.

It also has **rhythm** – repeating beats of sound and silence.

Music can be a simple tune, or a full-sized symphony with many **different layers** of sound.

It is often used to **celebrate** special occasions, such as weddings.

Music works well with **words**. We call these songs, or operas.

People enjoy **moving** to music to create dance.

You can listen to music when it is being performed at a concert or a gig. Or you can listen to recorded music whenever you like on your phone or computer.

Music can affect how people feel.

Think about an adventure film – upbeat background music helps to make you to feel **excited**.

What about a sad film? Slow string music can help to emphasise an **emotional** scene.

When did music start?

Music has been around for as long as humans have.
It started as a way for people to communicate.
The first musical instruments we know of come
from the Paleolithic Age. Say it like this:

PAY-lee-OH-li-thic

Flutes carved from vulture bones were found in caves
in Germany, which also had Ice Age wall paintings.
Those flutes are over 33,000 years old.

Prehistoric people made instruments from whatever was around them. Conch shells, bamboo canes, hollow wood, or even animal horns, were turned into something that could make a tune.

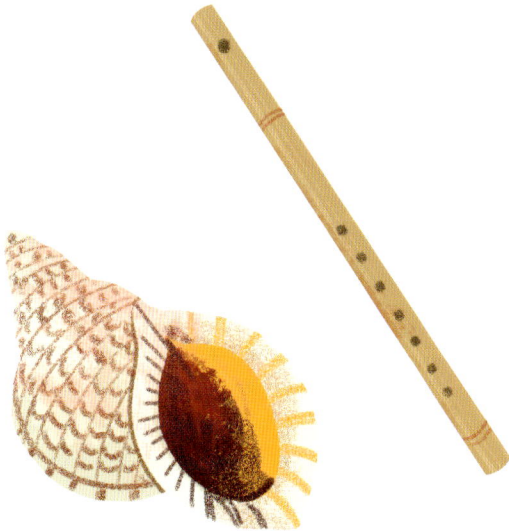

The earliest trumpet made from silver was found in **Tutankhamun's tomb**. This pharaoh ruled Egypt during the 14th century BCE.

The ancient Greeks made trumpets from **ivory and bronze** in the 5th century BCE.

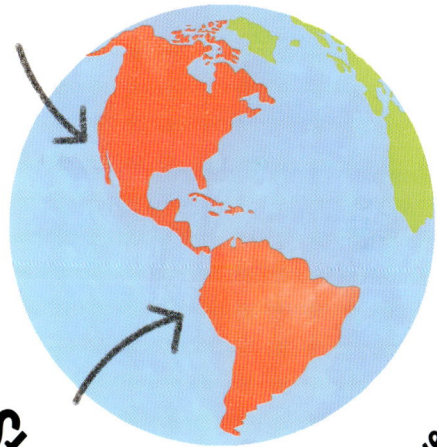

String instruments have not lasted as well, but by the end of the 11th century CE, the only part of the world that didn't have stringed instruments was the Americas.

Are there different types of music?

Until the late 19th century, music was either what is now called 'classical', which was heard by the upper classes in concert halls, or it came from the troubadour tradition. Troubadours travelled the land, using songs to spread news of events or famous people. This 'folk music' was listened to by the workers.

In the early 20th century, popular music was played on **record players** and then the radio.

This popular music came in many different forms and has led to the **huge variety** of music we enjoy today.

Classical

Jazz

Motown

Rock

Disco

Pop

Country

Reggae

Rap

Now we can listen to all sorts of music at the touch of a button. What do you like to listen to?

What is a song?

A song is a piece of music performed by a **voice**.

Songs have a **structure**. Most songs have verses with a repeated chorus.

A song featuring two singers singing together is called a **duet**.

A song can be sung **only** with the voice, or accompanied by musical instruments.

Different cultures have **different singing styles.**

A large group of singers is called
a **choir** and they sing all kinds of
music, from religious hymns to pop songs.

There are many **types of song**:
a carol, a nursery rhyme, a ballad,
a lullaby or a marching song.

tzz tzz
bup bup

Some singers use their voice
to **create noises** that
sound like percussion instruments.

11

What are musical instruments?

A musical instrument is simply an object that makes music. You can make music from anything, including sticks and stones.

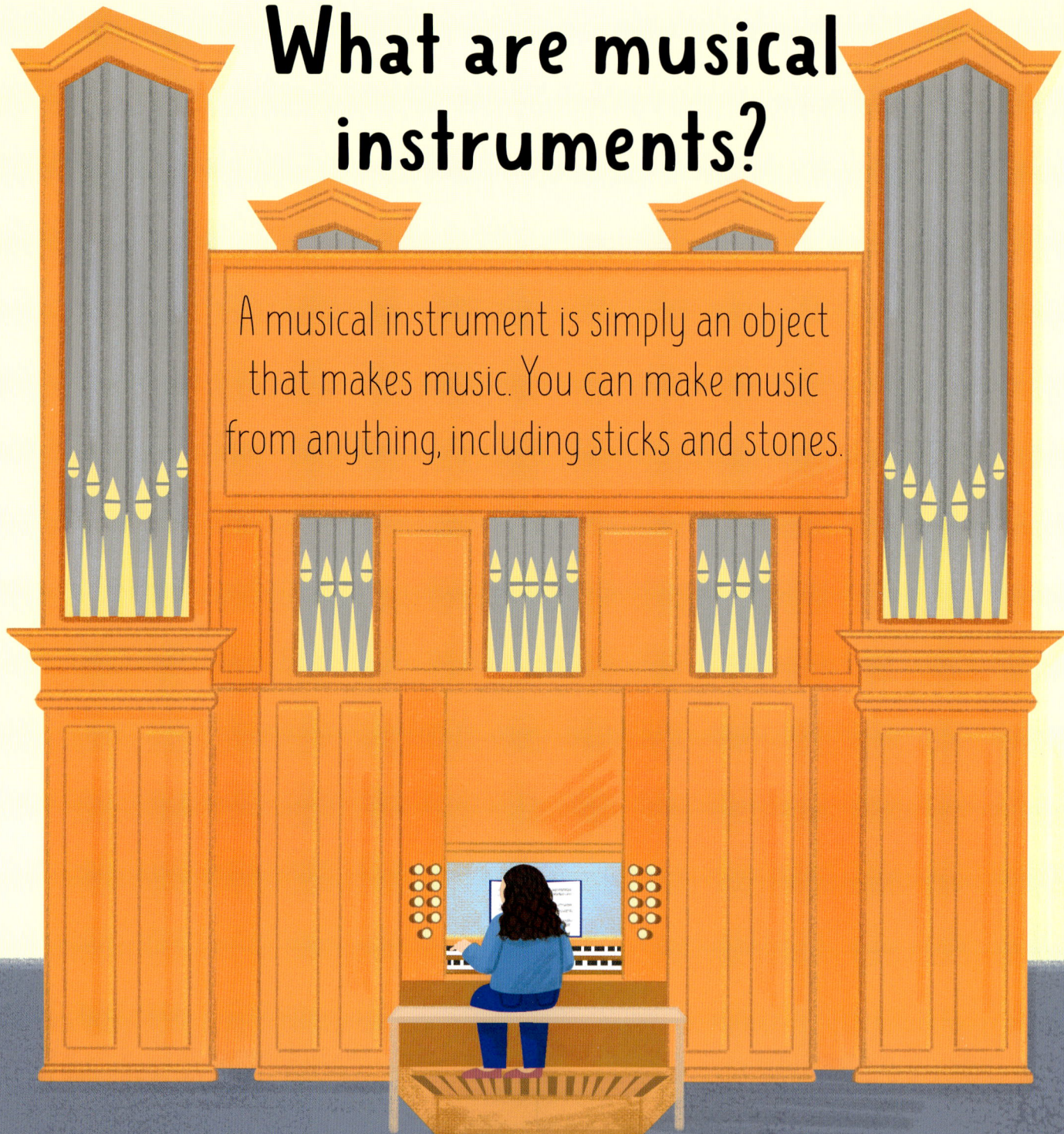

These days, musical instruments can be simple, such as a bell or whistle, or complicated, such as a pipe organ.

The **brass family** includes trumpets, trombones, horns and the tuba.

Some stringed instruments, such as the violin and cello, are played using a **bow**.

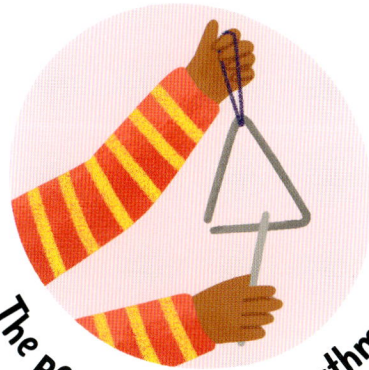

Guitars and banjos have **frets** to help the musician find the right note.

The percussion – or rhythm – section includes drums, cymbals, xylophones and the **triangle**.

The **wind family** includes flutes, piccolos and the reed family, such as the oboe or bassoon.

What is a choir?

A choir is an organised group of singers who perform in public. It can often be split into sections based on whether the singers can sing high or low notes. These sections of the choir sing different parts in harmony.

TENOR
(mid-low voices)

BASS
(low voices)

SOPRANO
(high voices)

ALTO
(mid-high voices)

Harmony is when two or more musical notes are played at the same time to make a **pleasing** sound.

There are many different types of choir.
Why don't you start one at your school?

A church choir sings hymns during church services. A **gospel choir** uses modern musical styles to bring energy and joy to the songs they sing.

A show choir often combines **song and dance** to put on a performance.

A **rock choir** sings popular rock songs with harmonies.

A barbershop choir, or quartet, often sings **a cappella**, which means they sing in close harmony without any musical instruments.

What is an orchestra?

An orchestra is a group of musicians who play music together. Usually, an orchestra has different sections – a string section, a wind section and a brass section, as well as a percussion section.

piccolo

French horn

flute

violin

conductor

A conductor helps the orchestral players stay in time with each other, as well as directing the musicians' performance.

percussion

timpani

oboe

bassoon

trombone

clarinet

tuba

trumpet

viola

cello

double bass

Orchestras usually play **classical music**, but can also be used in pop and rock music, or to produce film and TV soundtracks.

What is a composer?

A composer writes the music that orchestras and musicians play. They are often very good musicians themselves.

Another way to describe what they do is to say that they **arrange** music. An arrangement could be a different version of an existing song.

Songwriters also compose music. Sometimes they ask another person to help them write the words.

Here are some famous **classical composers.**
Not all were well-known in their own lifetimes.

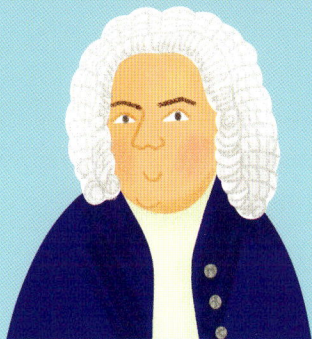

Johann Sebastian Bach

Ludwig van Beethoven

George Frideric Handel

Fanny Mendelssohn

Wolfgang Amadeus Mozart

Florence Price

Franz Schubert

Pyotr Ilyich Tchaikovsky

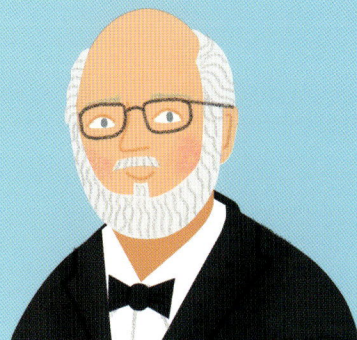

John Williams

Is music the same all around the world?

Different cultures have very different styles of music. They also have their own musical instruments..

African musicians are famous for their **drums and flutes**, but also play zithers, harps, lutes and lyres.

Islamic music is usually performed by **one singer**, who often improvises – makes up on the spot – within the piece.

The **Korean drum**, *changgo*, is hourglass shaped, with two sides. The left side is beaten with the player's hand and the right with a stick.

Polynesian music is closely linked with dancing, and often the performer will pretend to be a **mythical being** by wearing a mask and elaborate costume.

Chinese music can be traced back to **3000** BCE. Their **famous operas** date from the 12th century, but *jingxi*, known as Peking opera, is the most popular form.

The *shakuhachi* is a Japanese flute which is played as you would a recorder. In the past, the flute could also be used as a **weapon**.

Folk music is a part of daily life in rural India, where people sing while they work.

Have computers changed the world of music?

Music used to be stored on vinyl records, cassette tapes or compact discs, known as CDs. Some people still like to listen to records, but most people now use apps to **stream** songs or music they like from their computer or their smartphone.

Computers have also changed how music is created. In 1968, computer programmers built a tool or system that could control a **synthesizer** or electronic keyboard.

This was the start of **digital music**. Now composers, music producers and sound engineers can use computer programmes to make amazing music.

Computers can be used to transform music from sound into a **printed version** for musicians to play from.

Computers also allow musicians to **play live** together, even when they are in different parts of the world.

Scientists are also investigating whether a computer can actually **compose** music by itself.

Computers have changed how we make music and are essential to our ability to listen to and share music.

What can you do with music?

There are many ways you can use music in your life.

You can simply **enjoy** listening to music.

You can join a choir and sing **out loud**.

You can learn how to play a musical instrument and **join** a band or an orchestra.

You can watch a gig or go to a **concert**.

There are also lots of careers that involve music, even if you aren't a musician or singer yourself.

A music teacher helps people **learn** how to play an instrument or sing.

A music journalist **reports** on the music industry.

A concert promoter **organises** events for people to see their favourite musicians.

A sound engineer works with musicians to make their **recordings** sound amazing.

A radio DJ broadcasts shows on the radio and may create **podcasts.**

A music therapist uses music to **help people** with illnesses such as anxiety or memory loss.

Which career would you like to do when you grow up?

How does music help people?

Music is not just a pleasing sound to listen to. It also is good for you.

Listening to music reduces feelings of stress and anxiety.

It can make you **calm** ...

... or it can make you **dance**.

Certain types of music can improve your ability to learn and remember things.

Listening to music can **boost** your creativity and ability to solve problems.

It can also help you to finish a task or **reach a goal**.

Music can help you **sleep**.

Playing music with others means **sharing** in a positive experience.

Playing music is good for your **confidence**.

Playing music in a band or singing in a choir can help you make **friends**.

Music makes you happier.

So ... do we know what music is?

Music is an essential part of human life. It makes us feel good.

We know WHEN music started.

We understand what a SONG is.

We know the different types of MUSICAL INSTRUMENT.

We recognise different musical GENRES.

We know what a CHOIR and an ORCHESTRA are.

We know that COMPUTERS are really helpful in music production.

Not everyone can play a musical instrument or hold a tune when singing, but we know that nearly everyone can enjoy listening to music and feel happy.

Why don't you think about what you would like to do with music in the future?

Glossary

Anxiety a feeling of unease or worry

Accompany to play a musical instrument in support of a solo singer or musician

Ballad a slow and sentimental song

Bronze a yellowish-brown metal made from copper and tin

Carol a popular hymn sung at Christmas time

Celebrate to mark a significant event

Chorus a part of a song which is repeated after each verse

Concert a public musical performance

Culture humans' intellectual accomplishments, such as literature or history

Elaborate detailed and complicated in design or finish

Emotional feeling strongly about something

Emphasise to give special importance to something

Folk music traditional popular music

Fret a series of ridges on a stringed instrument that help you find a musical note

Gig a live music performance

Gospel music a passionate style of religious singing

Harp a framed musical instrument with parallel strings

Ice Age a period of time between 2.4 million years ago and 11,500 years ago when the Earth was extremely cold

Improvise to create music on the spot without preparation

Ivory the tusk of an elephant, walrus or narwhal used to make piano keys

Lullaby a gentle song sung to help children sleep

Lute a stringed instrument with frets and a round body with a flat front

Lyre a U-shaped harp

Melody — single notes arranged in a tune that is musically pleasant

Mythical — featured in myths and legends

Occasion — a particular event

Opera — a dramatic performance set to music

Pharaoh — a ruler in ancient Egypt

Podcast — a digital audio programme that can be listened to on a computer or mobile phone

Polynesia — a group of over 1,000 islands in the central and southern Pacific Ocean

Popular music — music that appeals to lots of people

Radio — a device that receives broadcast radio programmes and plays them in the home

Record player — a turntable that plays a record and amplifies the sound through a speaker

Structure — an organised arrangement of something

Symphony — an elaborate piece of music played by a full orchestra, usually in four movements

To direct — to control and manage

Troubadour — a poet who writes verse to music

Tune — a group of single notes arranged to sound pleasant

Verse — a group of lines that form a section in a song, often followed by a chorus

Vinyl — a man-made plastic used to make records

Vulture — a large bird of prey, whose bones were once used to make musical instruments

Zither — a flat, stringed instrument played horizontally, with strings that are plucked with fingers or a plectrum

With thanks to Rachel Bee, music teacher extraordinaire, who read the text and made some very sensible improvements.